M000121959

Alfred's INSTRUMENTAL CD+ INSIDE PLAY-ALONG

billboard
TOP TRACKS
Instrumental Solos

Last Week	This Week	Title CERTIFICATION PRODUCER [SONGWRITER]	Artist IMPRINT/PROMOTION LABEL
1	1	**#1** **8 WKS** **All About That Bass** KEVIN KADISH [M.TRAINOR, K.KADISH]	**Meghan Trainor** EPIC
2	2	**Firework** STARGATE, SANDY VEE [K.PERRY, M.ERIKSEN, T.E.HERMANSEN, S.WILHELM, E.DEAN]	**Katy Perry** CAPITOL
7	3	**Cool Kids** MIKE ELIZONDO [G.SIEROTA, J.SIEROTA, N.SIEROTA, S.SIEROTA, J.D.SIEROTA, J.DZWONEK]	**Echosmith** WARNER BROS.
6	4	**Best Day of My Life** AARON ACCETTA, SHEP GOODMAN [Z.BARNETT, J.A.SHELLEY, M.SANCHEZ, D.RUBLIN, S.GOODMAN, A.ACCETTA]	**American Authors** MERCURY/ISLAND
5	5	**Grenade** THE SMEEZINGTONS [C.KELLY, B.BROWN, P.LAWRENCE, A.LEVINE, A.WYATT, B.MARS]	**Bruno Mars** ATLANTIC/ELEKTRA
8	6	**Payphone** SHELLBACK, B.BLANCO [W.KHALIFA, A.LEVINE, B.LEVIN, A.MALIK, J.SCHUSTER, D.OMELIO]	**Maroon 5** Feat. Wiz Khalifa A&M/OCTONE
6	7	**Let It Go** K.ANDERSON-LOPEZ, R.LOPEZ, C.BECK, C.MONTAN, T.MACDOUGALL [K.ANDERSON-LOPEZ, R.LOPEZ]	**Frozen** WALT DISNEY RECORDS
12	8	**Problem** MAX MARTIN, ILYA, SHELLBACK [I.SALMANZADEH, MAX MARTIN, S.KOTECHA, A. KELLY, A.GRANDE]	**Ariana Grande** Feat. Iggy Azalea REPUBLIC
10	9	**Ain't It Fun** JUSTIN MELDAL-JOHNSEN [H.WILLIAMS, T.YORK]	**Paramore** FUELED BY RAMEN/WARNER BROS.
11	10	**Need You Now** LADY ANTEBELLUM, PAUL WORLEY [D.HAYWOOD, C.KELLEY, H.SCOTT, J.KEAR]	**Lady Antebellum** NASHVILLE
11	11	**Domino** DR. LUKE, CIRKUT [C.KELLY, L.GOTTWALD, M.MARTIN...]	**Jessie J**

Arranged by Bill Galliford and Ethan Neuburg.
Recordings produced by Dan Warner, Doug Emery, and Lee Levin.

© 2015 Alfred Music
All Rights Reserved. Printed in USA.

ISBN-10: 1-4706-2374-9
ISBN-13: 978-1-4706-2374-6

Title CERTIFICATION
PRODUCER (SONGWRITER)
IMPRINT/F

Week

#1
8 WKS All About That Bass
KEVIN KADISH (M.TRAINOR,K,KADISH)

Meg

Song ARTIST	Page	mp3 CD Demo	Track Play-Along
Tuning Note (B♭ Concert)			1
All About That Bass Meghan Trainor	4	2	3
We Are Young fun.	7	4	5
Let It Go from Walt Disney's *Frozen*	10	6	7
In My Head Jason Derulo	13	8	9
Firework Katy Perry	16	10	11
Payphone Maroon 5 Feat. Wiz Khalifa	18	12	13
Just the Way You Are (Amazing) Bruno Mars	20	14	15
Need You Now Lady Antebellum	22	16	17
Grenade Bruno Mars	24	18	19
Smile Uncle Kracker	26	20	21
Part of Me Katy Perry	28	22	23

Title CERTIFICATION
PRODUCER [SONGWRITER]

IMPRINT/PRO

#1
8 WKS
All About That Bass
KEVIN KADISH [M.TRAINOR,K.KADISH]

Megha

K

E-

Song ARTIST	Page	mp3 cd Track Demo	Play-Along
Good Time Owl City and Carly Rae Jepsen	30	24	25
Domino Jessie J	32	26	27
Problem Ariana Grande Feat. Iggy Azalea	34	28	29
Ain't It Fun Paramore	36	30	31
Everything Is Awesome (Awesome Remixxx!!!) from The Lego Movie	38	32	33
Me and My Broken Heart Rixton	40	34	35
Best Day of My Life American Authors	42	36	37
Stay the Night Zedd Feat. Hayley Williams	44	38	39
Daylight Maroon 5	46	40	41
Just Give Me A Reason Pink Feat. Nate Ruess	48	42	43
Cool Kids Echosmith	50	44	45
Roar Katy Perry	51	46	47

ALL ABOUT THAT BASS

Track 2: Demo
Track 3: Play-Along

Words and Music by
MEGHAN TRAINOR and KEVIN KADISH

Moderately bright (♩ = 132)

All About That Bass - 3 - 1

6

WE ARE YOUNG

Track 4: Demo
Track 5: Play-Along

Words and Music by
NATE RUESS, JEFF BHASKER,
ANDREW DOST and JACK ANTONOFF

We Are Young - 3 - 1

8

62 *Bridge:*

To Coda ⊕

1.

2.

D.S. % al Coda

⊕ *Coda*

mp

From Walt Disney's Frozen

LET IT GO

Track 6: Demo
Track 7: Play-Along

Music and Lyrics by
KRISTEN ANDERSON-LOPEZ
and ROBERT LOPEZ

Let It Go - 3 - 1

Let It Go - 3 - 2

12

IN MY HEAD

Track 8: Demo
Track 9: Play-Along

Words and Music by
CLAUDE KELLY, JONATHAN ROTEM
and JASON DESROULEAUX

Moderate pop rock (♩ = 112)

5 *Verse:*

21 *Chorus:*

In My Head - 3 - 1

FIREWORK

Track 10: Demo
Track 11: Play-Along

Words and Music by
KATY PERRY, MIKKEL ERIKSEN,
TOR ERIK HERMANSEN, SANDY WILHELM
and ESTER DEAN

Firework - 2 - 1

46 *Bridge:*

54 *Chorus:*

70

PAYPHONE

Track 12: Demo
Track 13: Play-Along

Words and Music by
WIZ KHALIFA, ADAM LEVINE,
BENJAMIN LEVIN, AMMAR MALIK,
JOHAN SCHUSTER and DANIEL OMELIO

Payphone - 2 - 1

19

Payphone - 2 - 2

JUST THE WAY YOU ARE (AMAZING)

Track 14: Demo
Track 15: Play-Along

Words and Music by
KHALIL WALTON, PETER HERNANDEZ,
PHILIP LAWRENCE, ARI LEVINE
and KHARI CAIN

Moderately (♩ = 112)

Just the Way You Are (Amazing) - 2 - 1

NEED YOU NOW

Track 16: Demo
Track 17: Play-Along

Words and Music by
DAVE HAYWOOD, CHARLES KELLEY,
HILLARY SCOTT and JOSH KEAR

Moderately (♩ = 108)

Need You Now - 2 - 1

To Coda ⊕

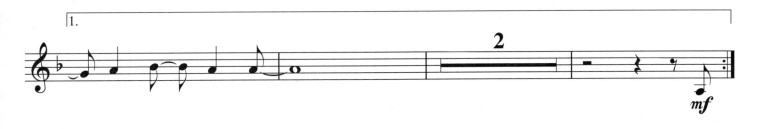

D.S. 𝄋 al Coda

⊕ *Coda*

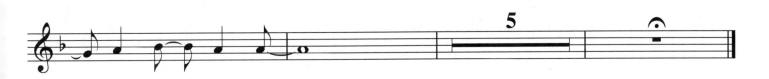

Need You Now - 2 - 2

GRENADE

Track 18: Demo
Track 19: Play-Along

Words and Music by
CLAUDE KELLY, BRODY BROWN,
PHILIP LAWRENCE, ARI LEVINE,
ANDREW WYATT and BRUNO MARS

Moderately (♩ = 112)

Grenade - 2 - 1

SMILE

Track 20: Demo
Track 21: Play-Along

Words and Music by
MATTHEW SHAFER, BLAIR DALY,
J.T. HARDING and JEREMY BOSE

Slow groove, half-time feel ($\quarternote$ = 72)

Smile - 2 - 1

PART OF ME

Track 22: Demo
Track 23: Play-Along

Words and Music by
KATY PERRY, LUKASZ GOTTWALD,
MAX MARTIN and BONNIE McKEE

Medium dance tempo (♩ = 132)

Part of Me - 2 - 1

Track 24: Demo
Track 25: Play-Along

GOOD TIME

Words and Music by
MATTHEW THIESSEN, BRIAN LEE
and ADAM YOUNG

Moderate dance tempo (♩ = 120)

Good Time - 2 - 1

DOMINO

Track 26: Demo
Track 27: Play-Along

Words and Music by
CLAUDE KELLY, LUKASZ GOTTWALD,
MAX MARTIN, HENRY WALTER
and JESSICA CORNISH

Moderate dance rock (♩ = 120)

Domino - 2 - 1

PROBLEM

Track 28: Demo
Track 29: Play-Along

Words and Music by
ILYA, ARIANA GRANDE, MAX MARTIN,
AMETHYST AMELIA KELLY and SAVAN KOTECHA

Moderate dance rock (♩ = 103)

Problem - 2 - 1

AIN'T IT FUN

Track 30: Demo
Track 31: Play-Along

Words and Music by
HAYLEY WILLIAMS and TAYLOR YORK

Moderate rock (♩ = 104)

5 *Verse:*

13

21 *Chorus:*

Ain't It Fun - 2 - 1

Ain't It Fun - 2 - 2

From The LEGO® Movie

EVERYTHING IS AWESOME
(AWESOME REMIXXX!!!)

Track 32: Demo
Track 33: Play-Along

Lyrics by
SHAWN PATTERSON, ANDY SAMBERG,
AKIVA SCHAFFER, JORMA TACCONE,
JOSHUA BARTHOLOMEW and LISA HARRITON

Music by
SHAWN PATTERSON

Very bright (♩ = 154)

Everything Is Awesome (Awesome Remixxx!!!) - 2 - 1

Everything Is Awesome (Awesome Remixxx!!!) - 2 - 2

ME AND MY BROKEN HEART

Track 34: Demo
Track 35: Play-Along

Words and Music by
WAYNE HECTOR, STEVE MAC,
BENJAMIN LEVIN, AMMAR MALIK
and ROB THOMAS

Moderate pop (♩ = 88) *Chorus:*

Me and My Broken Heart - 2 - 1

Me and My Broken Heart - 2 - 2

BEST DAY OF MY LIFE

Track 36: Demo
Track 37: Play-Along

Words and Music by
ZACHARY BARNETT, JAMES ADAM SHELLEY,
MATTHEW SANCHEZ, DAVID RUBLIN,
SHEP GOODMAN and AARON ACCETTA

Moderate rock (♩ = 96)

Best Day of My Life - 2 - 1

STAY THE NIGHT

Track 38: Demo
Track 39: Play-Along

Words and Music by
BENJAMIN HANNA, HAYLEY WILLIAMS,
CARAH FAYE and ANTON ZASLAVSKI

Moderately bright (♩ = 126)

Stay the Night - 2 - 1

DAYLIGHT

Track 40: Demo
Track 41: Play-Along

Words and Music by
SAM MARTIN, MASON LEVY,
ADAM LEVINE and MAX MARTIN

Moderate rock (♩ = 120)

JUST GIVE ME A REASON

Track 42: Demo
Track 43: Play-Along

Words and Music by
NATE RUESS, ALECIA MOORE
and JEFF BHASKER

Just Give Me a Reason - 2 - 1

COOL KIDS

Words and Music by
GRAHAM SIEROTA, JAMIE SIEROTA,
NOAH SIEROTA, SYDNEY SIEROTA,
JEFFERY DAVID SIEROTA and JESIAH DZWONEK

ROAR

Words and Music by
KATY PERRY, BONNIE McKEE,
MAX MARTIN, LUKASZ GOTTWALD
and HENRY WALTER

PARTS OF THE HORN AND FINGERING CHART

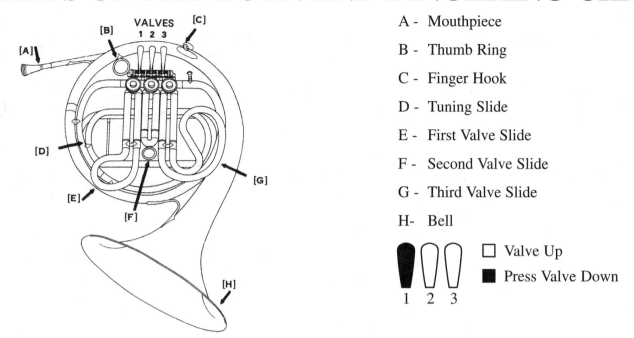

A - Mouthpiece

B - Thumb Ring

C - Finger Hook

D - Tuning Slide

E - First Valve Slide

F - Second Valve Slide

G - Third Valve Slide

H- Bell

☐ Valve Up

■ Press Valve Down

F Horns use the top fingerings. B♭ Horns use the bottom fingerings. F/B♭ Double Horns use the top fingerings without the thumb, or the bottom fingerings with the thumb. A good rule is to play notes from the second line G down on the F Horn, and from the second line G♯ up on the B♭ Horn.

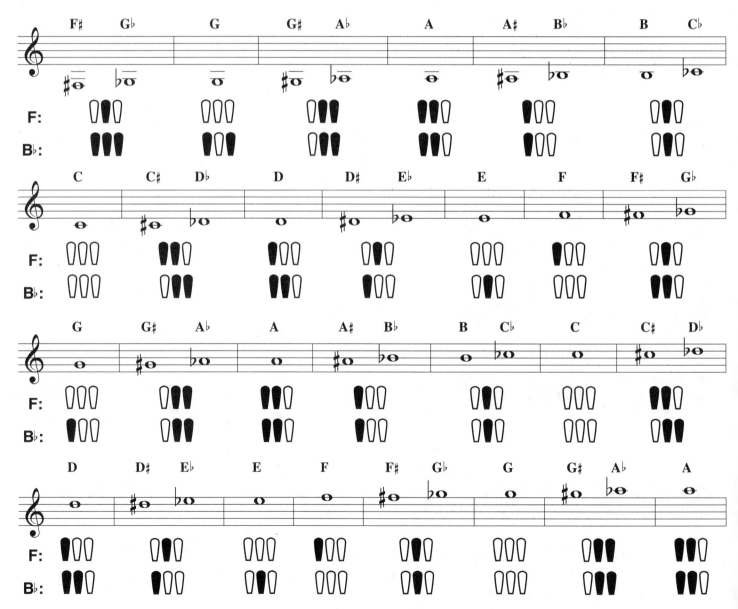

ROAR

Track 46: Demo
Track 47: Play-Along

Words and Music by
KATY PERRY, BONNIE McKEE,
MAX MARTIN, LUKASZ GOTTWALD
and HENRY WALTER

Moderate pop rock (♩ = 90)

PARTS OF THE HORN AND FINGERING CHART

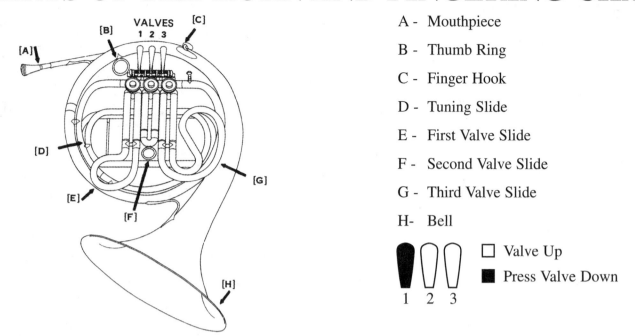

A - Mouthpiece

B - Thumb Ring

C - Finger Hook

D - Tuning Slide

E - First Valve Slide

F - Second Valve Slide

G - Third Valve Slide

H- Bell

☐ Valve Up
■ Press Valve Down

F Horns use the top fingerings. B♭ Horns use the bottom fingerings. F/B♭ Double Horns use the top fingerings without the thumb, or the bottom fingerings with the thumb. A good rule is to play notes from the second line G down on the F Horn, and from the second line G♯ up on the B♭ Horn.

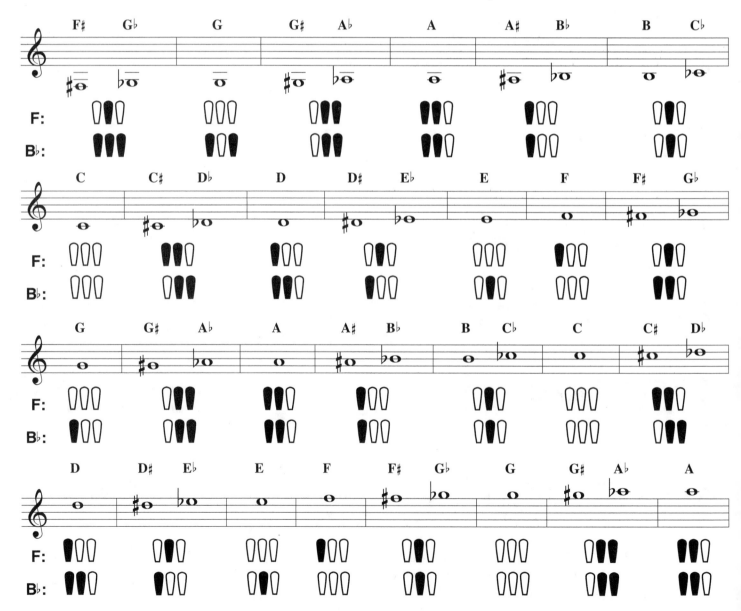